SUPER SMART INFORMATION STRATEGIES

CREATING DIGITAL BROCHURES

by Heather Newman

CHERRY LAKE PUBLISHING • ANN ARBOR, MICHIGAN

A NOTE TO PARENTS AND TEACHERS: Please remind your children how to stay safe online before they do the activities in this book.

A NOTE TO KIDS: Always remember your safety comes first!

CHERRY LAKE Publishing

Published in the United States of America
by Cherry Lake Publishing
Ann Arbor, Michigan
www.cherrylakepublishing.com

Content Adviser: Gail Dickinson, PhD, Associate Professor, Old Dominion University, Norfolk, Virginia

Photo Credits: Cover, ©sebra/Shutterstock, Inc.; page 4, © imagebroker/Alamy; page 5, ©Jeff Greenberg/Alamy; page 7, ©Anthony Baggett/Dreamstime.com; page 9, ©woodleywonderworks / www.flickr.com / CC-BY-2.0; page 10, ©Michael Wick/ Shutterstock, Inc.; page 11, ©Alex E. Proimos / www.flickr.com / CC-BY-2.0; page 12, ©val lawless/Shutterstock, Inc.; page 15, ©Aislinn Ritchie / www.flickr.com / CC-BY-SA-2.0; page 16, courtesy of Michigan Makers; page 17, ©Barrett.Discovery / www.flickr.com / CC-BY-2.0; page 18, ©Khomulo Anna/Shutterstock, Inc.; page 19 top left, ©Andres Moreira / www.flickr.com / CC-BY-SA-2.0; page 19 top right, ©Matthew Collingwood/ Dreamstime; page 19 bottom, ©andreaarden / www.flickr.com / CC-BY-2.0; page 21, ©NASA Goddard Photo and Video / www.flickr.com / CC-BY-2.0; pages 23 and 26, ©Pressmaster/Shutterstock, Inc.; page 25, ©kjarrett / www.flickr.com / CC-BY-2.0

Library of Congress Cataloging-in-Publication Data
Newman, Heather, 1970–
Creating digital brochures / by Heather Newman.
pages cm. — (Information explorer)
Includes bibliographical references and index.
ISBN 978-1-62431-128-4 (lib. bdg.) — ISBN 978-1-62431-260-1 (pbk.) — ISBN 978-1-62431-194-9 (e-book)
1. Brochures—Design—Juvenile literature. 2. Graphic design (Typography)—Data processing—Juvenile literature. I. Title.

Z246.5.B76N49 2014
686.2'2—dc23

2013011336

Cherry Lake Publishing would like to acknowledge the work of The Partnership for 21st Century Skills. Please visit *www.p21.org* for more information.

Printed in the United States of America
Corporate Graphics Inc.
July 2013
CLFA13

Table of Contents

4 Chapter One
What Is a Digital Brochure?

9 Chapter Two
What's Your Message?

15 Chapter Three
Picking Out Pictures

21 Chapter Four
Putting It Together

26 Chapter Five
Sharing Your Brochure with the World

30 Glossary
31 Find Out More
32 Index
32 About the Author

CHAPTER ONE

What Is a Digital Brochure?

Brochures are often used to advertise tourist attractions to travelers.

Have you ever seen a display rack filled with bright pictures printed on folded paper? Those folded papers are brochures. You might find them in rest stops along a highway or near the entrances to stores. These brochures might advertise things to do or places to eat. But brochures can be used for many other purposes as well.

Have you ever wanted to tell people about a project you're working on? Perhaps you wanted to encourage people to do something important, like take steps to save the environment. Or you were holding a fund-raiser for your school or club and needed to tell people why they should chip in. Maybe you started a small business selling things and wanted to let people know about the work you do. These are just some things that brochures are good for.

Brochures use words and pictures to provide information. They tell readers about a topic and encourage them to do something. It could be to donate to a charity, join a group, visit a new town, or participate in a new activity. Brochures are often printed. However, you can also make digital brochures using a word processing or desktop publishing program on your computer. You can e-mail these digital brochures to people or post them on a Web site.

Printed brochures are useful for providing information to people who are away from their computers.

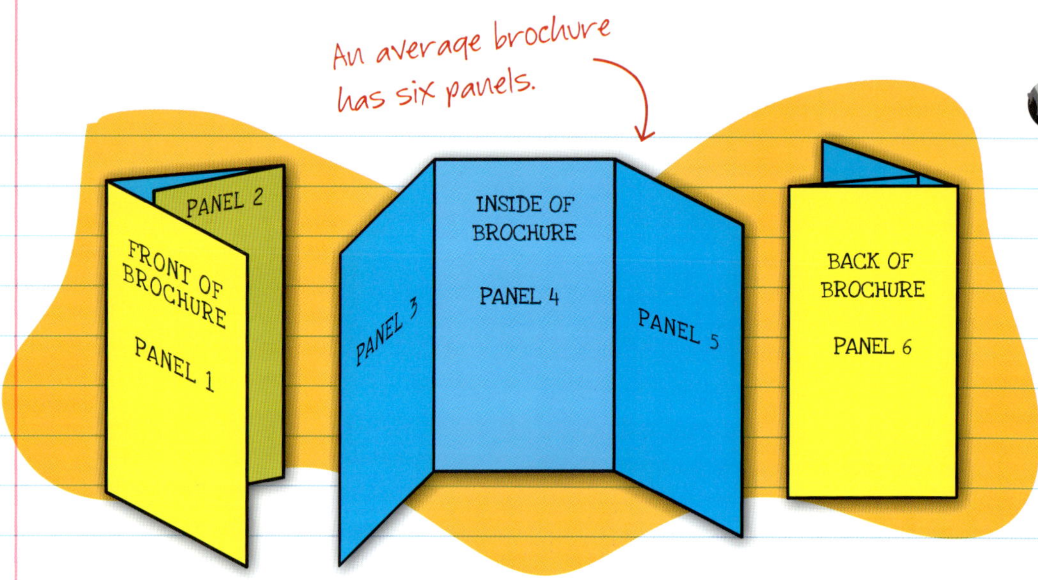

Brochures come in many shapes and sizes, but the most common type is a single piece of letter-sized paper, folded in thirds. This is called a trifold brochure, because the paper is folded into three sections. It is a good size for many projects, and it uses paper that is easy to find. Folding a piece of paper into thirds gives you six sections for your brochure. You'll end up with a front cover that takes up one-third of one side of the paper and attracts people to your brochure, a back cover where you restate your most important points, and four other sections where you put more information.

That sounds like a lot of space, but it's not. Trifold brochures have room for only about 15 to 20 sentences, especially if you include pictures. You'll want to make sure that's enough room to explain everything you want to say. A brochure might have too much space for simple things, such as inviting people to an event. In that case, you need only a few words describing the occasion, along with the date, time, and location.

Posters are a great way to advertise simple messages.

There are many other ways to tell people about your project or topic. If you don't have a lot to say, you might want to try a **flyer** or a poster. These usually have only a few words and one or two pictures on a single unfolded page. If you have more things to say than you can fit on the six sections of a brochure, you might want to think about making a booklet or a Web site. These can hold far more information than a brochure can. But if what you have to say fits into a brochure, it's a great way to present your words in a format that's easy for people to read and hold.

TRY THIS!

There are many reasons to make a brochure. Here are a few examples:

- You are starting a new club.
- You are raising money for a charity.
- You want to tell people about a great restaurant or tourist attraction in your town.
- You want to tell people about your favorite animal.
- You want to show your friends how to recycle.
- You want to get more members for your after-school group.
- You want to tell people about another country.
- You want to tell people how to make a fancy meal.

Make a list of topics that you might want to create a brochure for. Check off those that you think you could describe in 15 to 20 sentences. Now pick your three favorites. You'll use these choices to get started!

To get a copy of this activity, visit www.cherrylakepublishing.com/activities.

CHAPTER TWO

What's Your Message?

You will need to think carefully about which information to include on each panel.

Your brochure has a limited amount of space. You have room for only about 15 to 20 sentences. You'll need to pick and choose carefully what you want to say. Every sentence you use should help get your point across. Your words will teach, encourage, or request something from the people who read them. To help figure out what your 15 to 20 sentences will say, break them down into four parts: introduction, problem, solution, and call to action.

Introduction

Your introduction is the part that tells people what your brochure is about. It starts on the front cover, where you put one or two sentences. For example, a brochure about leopards might start by describing what a leopard is and why you chose to write about it. If you're writing about a club you belong to, you might tell readers the name of the group and when it meets. You'll also put a title and perhaps a picture or two on the front cover.

A brochure about leopards might include information about their spotted fur.

The problem section of your brochure might describe the ways trash hurts plants and animals.

Problem

You usually make a brochure because you need to solve a problem. The problem might be that people don't know about something you think is important. For a brochure about a club, your problem might be that you don't have enough members. Maybe your problem is more complicated. For a brochure about recycling, the problem could be the effect that trash has on the environment. The problem section of your brochure lays out what people should know about the subject you're writing about. It includes facts and figures from sources you trust, basic information about your topic, and some ideas about why readers should care about what you have to say. The problem section is the biggest section of the brochure because it includes lots of information about your topic. It might include eight or nine sentences.

Solution

The solution is the fun part of the brochure. This is where you tell your readers how they can help and why they should! If the brochure is telling them about a group, this would be the section that explains how to join and what will happen when they do. If you're describing your band's performances, this would be where you tell people how to attend and what they'll see. If your brochure teaches readers how to do something, such as drawing a cartoon character, tell them how they can learn more and how they can teach their friends. This is usually the second-largest section of your brochure, so plan on devoting four or five sentences to the solution.

A brochure for your school marching band might tell people which parades it will be performing at and where they should stand to get the best view.

A call to action encourages your readers to do what your brochure asks them.

Call to Action

This part of your brochure is short but important. This is where you ask people to do what you described in the solution section. You might write, "Please join us!" if you're describing your band performances or your new club. You might write, "Learn more about leopards at the library or at this Web site!" if your brochure describes your favorite animal. This section should describe no more than three things you want people to do after reading your brochure. If the brochure describes how to draw a cartoon character, you could leave a space for them to draw right on the brochure and ask them to try it themselves! This section should be no more than three sentences long. Even a single sentence is fine.

To get a copy of this activity, visit www.cherrylakepublishing.com/activities.

TRY THIS!

Pick one of your three brochure ideas from chapter 1 and write down ideas for what to put in each of these parts: introduction, problem, solution, and call to action. Now write a few sentences for each part. Ask your friends and family to read it over when you're done.

Plan out a sample brochure before you create the final copy.

CHAPTER THREE

Picking Out Pictures

Taking your own photographs is a great way to customize your brochure.

Adding drawings or photographs to your brochure can help grab people's attention. The front and back sections of brochures often have large pictures so that people will see them and pick up the brochure to read it. Pictures are also useful to illustrate your points, so you don't have to explain everything with words. The next time you're in a place that has brochures (such as your doctor's office or the library), look at the front covers. Chances are good that these brochures have pictures.

You can also create your own artwork and scan it into your computer to use on a brochure.

You can get images for your brochure from many places. You can draw them yourself or use a drawing program on your computer. If you don't have a **scanner** to get your drawing into the computer, take a picture of it! You can also take photographs or find photos online.

Pictures belong to the people who took or drew them. Even if you find images somewhere public, like a Web site, that doesn't mean you can use them yourself. You might be breaking **copyright** law, which makes it illegal to use a picture or a story without the permission of the person who made it.

There are some pictures you can always use. You may use anything from a government Web site (a site that ends in *.gov* or *.us*) unless it has a credit that says it was created by someone who doesn't work for the government. You may also use pictures that have Creative Commons **licenses**. Creative Commons licenses are special permissions that allow you to use images and other creations as long as you give credit to the owner. Other sites online also offer free images. Ask an adult to help you find sites with images you can use in your brochure.

There are many Web sites where you can search for images to use in your brochures.

The best pictures draw your readers in and make them curious. When you're choosing photos, look for ones that include people. Everyone likes to see other people in photographs! Make sure your photographs are in focus. You also need to make sure the images you choose are big enough to look good when they come out of the printer. If an image is too small, it will look blurry when you print it. Look for the biggest photos you can find! You can always make them look smaller when you put them in your brochure.

Be sure to choose images that will look clear and colorful when they are printed out.

Don't use too many pictures in your brochure. Having one bigger drawing or photograph is better than having a lot of tiny ones. Too many images will make your brochure hard to read. It's also best not to mix drawings and photographs. Using all photographs or all drawings will look better on the page. Find or create four to five photos or drawings that you really like.

A large photo on the cover can have a big impact!

TRY THIS!

Make a list of all the pictures you would like to include in your brochure. Mark which photographs or drawings you could create yourself and which ones you might look for online. Now consider whether your readers will like those images. Take photos, make drawings, or look for images online that might match your topic. Then use this checklist to pick the best ones. Choose photos or drawings that do the following:

- Show something that you wrote about in the brochure
- Grab the viewer's attention right away
- Look sharp and crisp
- Look good when printed out
- Include people or animals
- Are pretty, unusual, or interesting
- Are free to use under copyright law

To get a copy of this activity, visit www.cherrylakepublishing.com/activities.

CHAPTER FOUR

Putting It Together

Most computers come with at least one word processing program that you can use to create your brochures.

There are many different computer programs you can use to create your brochure. Try a word processing program such as Microsoft Word or Apple Pages. Most word processing programs have brochure **templates**. Templates provide premade designs with places for you to insert text and images.

If you do not have a brochure template, you can simply make **columns**. (If you don't know how, ask an adult or search under the program's Help menu.) A simple brochure consists of two pages with three columns on each page. The pages should be sideways, with the long side on top. Most programs call this the landscape **orientation**. You can usually find the option to turn the page sideways under your program's Page Layout or Format menu.

Desktop publishing programs, such as Microsoft Publisher or Adobe InDesign, are made specifically to help organize words and pictures on printed pages. You

Make sure your columns are set up correctly before adding text or images.

Ask for opinions if you aren't sure about a font or color on your brochure.

can draw boxes on the page where you want your words and pictures to go. These programs usually take a little more work to learn than a word processing program.

There are lots of things to remember as you design your brochure. Before you start, be sure to change the page orientation to landscape. Make your text into three even columns on each page so you don't fold through the words when you fold up your brochure. Don't forget headlines. You'll want a big one on the front section (the right column of your first page) to tell people what your brochure is about. Change the **font** to bold and a bigger size for that!

You might want to include some smaller headlines in other parts of your brochure, especially for your call to action. Don't change the font too often, though. Too many changes will make your brochure hard to read. Two fonts are enough! Pick one for the text and another for the headlines. Put your pictures where you want them, and put tiny text under them that gives credit to whoever took them, even if it's you.

Hint: If you have trouble figuring out where the front and back sections of your brochure are, try folding up a blank piece of paper. Now look where each section lands on the page.

Make sure you put the correct text and images in each panel.

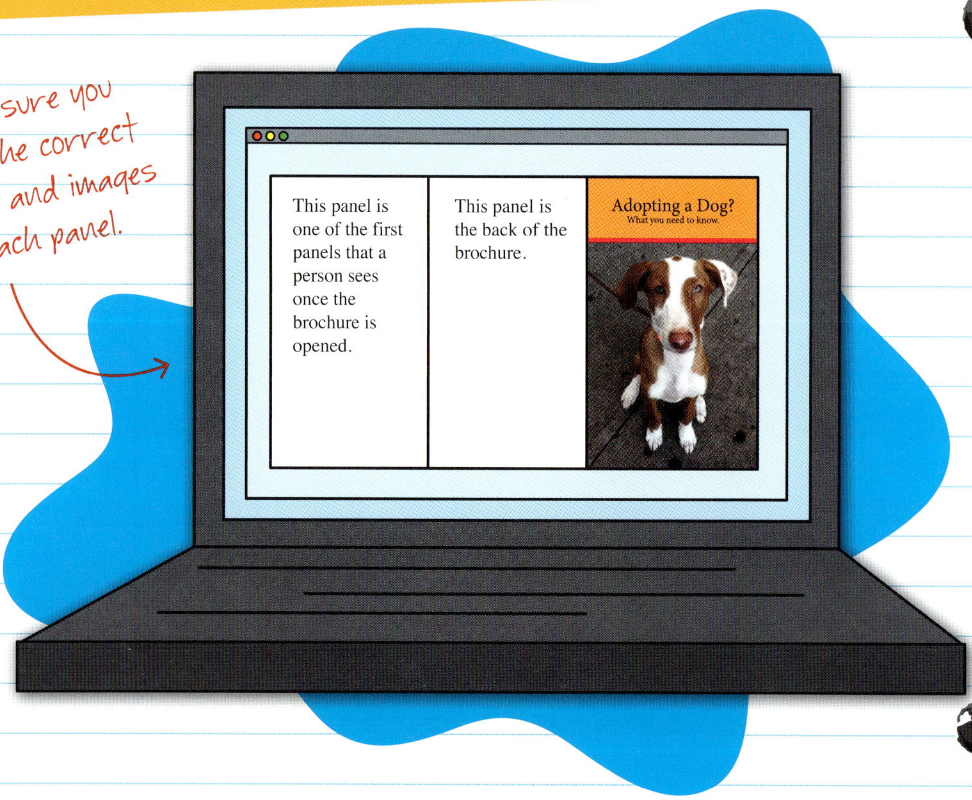

Chapter Four: Putting It Together

TRY THIS!

Pick a word processing or desktop publishing program on your computer. Or, with an adult's help, download or use a special brochure-making program online. Look at the brochure templates that are available. Choose the template that works best with your brochure. Put your text and the pictures you've chosen into the template. Don't forget headlines and photo credits!

To get a copy of this activity, visit www.cherrylakepublishing.com/activities.

CHAPTER FIVE

Sharing Your Brochure with the World

Your classmates might make the perfect audience for your brochure.

Congratulations! Your brochure is almost done. Once you have all of your text and images in place, print out a copy to see what it looks like on paper. You will need to print out one side of your brochure, then flip the paper around and put it back in your printer before printing the other side.

Now you need to decide who the audience for your brochure will be. Is it your friends at school? Other students? Teachers, family, or friends? Other people in your community? Figuring out who your audience is will help you figure out how to send it to people. Should you print it out and give people paper copies? That can be a waste of paper, which comes from trees. A better way might be to e-mail your brochure to people. But if you don't know people's e-mail addresses, sometimes paper is the only way. You might also be able to post it on a Web site.

If you choose to print your brochure, you'll need to know the following:

- How many copies you need
- Whether you'll use a copy machine or a printer
- Whether you will print in color or black and white (color is more expensive)
- Whether you want to hand out your brochures or leave them in a place where people will find them (ask permission first!)

If you decide to send your brochure by e-mail, you'll need to know the following:

- How to save the brochure in a file type that everyone can read (PDF files work well, and many programs can make them)
- How to attach the brochure to an e-mail message
- Your friends' e-mail addresses

Hint: Don't e-mail people you don't know, unless you are sure they want to see your brochure. Unwanted e-mail is called spam, and no one likes getting spam!

If you, your school, or your club has a Web site, you can post your brochure there. Ask for an adult's help anytime you post things online. Be sure you aren't including personal information, such as your address or phone number on anything that can be seen by strangers, whether it's online or on paper!

Ask local businesses if they will display your printed brochures.

TRY THIS!

Make a list of everyone you want to receive your brochure. This list might include friends and family, people involved in an activity with you, or people at your school or in your community. Make a list of pros and cons for giving the brochure to them on paper or online. How will you get their addresses? With your parents' or teacher's permission, e-mail the brochure to some people, and print it out for others.

Will you print in color or black-and-white?

To get a copy of this activity, visit www.cherrylakepublishing.com/activities.

Glossary

columns (KAH-luhmz) words and images arranged vertically

copyright (KAH-pee-rite) the legal right to control the use of something created, such as a song, book, or picture

flyer (FLY-ur) a paper advertisement

font (FAHNT) a style of type

licenses (LYE-suhn-siz) documents that officially grant permission for you to use or do something

orientation (or-ee-uhn-TAY-shuhn) the position of something or the direction something faces

scanner (SKAN-ur) a machine that uses a beam of light to copy an image or read information

templates (TEM-pluhts) documents or patterns that are used to create similar documents

Find Out More

BOOKS

Bernstein, Daryl. *Better Than a Lemonade Stand!: Small Business Ideas for Kids*. New York: Aladdin, 2012.

Cornwall, Phyllis. *Online Etiquette and Safety*. Ann Arbor, MI: Cherry Lake, 2011.

Truesdell, Ann. *Make Your Point: Creating Powerful Presentations*. Ann Arbor, MI: Cherry Lake, 2013.

WEB SITES

Brother Creative Center

www.brother.com/creativecenter/us/en_us/business/brochure

Create brochures online with your own words and pictures and then print them out on your computer.

wikiHow.com

www.wikihow.com/Make-Brochures-on-Microsoft-Word

This guide shows how to make a brochure using templates in Microsoft Word 2010, but you can use many of the same steps in other word processing programs.

Index

Adobe InDesign, 22–23
Apple Pages, 21
audience, 26–27, 29

back section, 15, 24

call to action, 13, 14, 24
columns, 22, 23
computer programs, 5, 16, 21–23, 25, 27
copyright laws, 16, 20
Creative Commons licenses, 17
credits, 17, 24, 25

design, 21, 23
desktop publishing programs, 5, 22–23, 25

e-mail, 5, 27–28, 29

flyers, 7
fonts, 23, 24
front section, 6, 10, 15, 23, 24

headlines, 23–24, 25

introduction section, 10, 14

landscape orientation, 22, 23

Microsoft Publisher, 22–23
Microsoft Word, 21

PDF files, 27
pictures, 6, 7, 10, 15–19, 20, 22–23, 24, 25
posters, 7
printing, 5, 18, 20, 26, 27, 29
problem section, 11, 14
projects, 4–5, 7, 8

sizes, 6, 23
solution section, 12, 13, 14
space, 6, 7, 9
spam, 28

templates, 21, 25
titles, 10
trifold brochures, 6

Web sites, 5, 7, 16, 17, 27, 28
word processing programs, 5, 21, 25

About the Author

Heather Newman is in charge of marketing at the University of Michigan School of Information, where she helps create dozens of different brochures every year.